INVENTORS

THE WRIGHT BROTHERS

PAUL JOSEPH
ABDO & Daughters

Published by Abdo & Daughters, 4940 Viking Drive, Suite 622, Edina, Minnesota 55435.

Cover illustration and icon: Kristen Copham
Interior photos: Bettmann, pages 5, 7, 16, 19, 25
                    Archive Photos, pages 9, 15, 29
                    Wide World Photos, page 27
Photo colorization: Professional Litho

Edited by Bob Italia

Library of Congress Cataloging-in-Publication Data

Joseph, Paul, 1970-
The Wright brothers / Paul Joseph.
   p. cm. — (Inventors)
Includes index.
Summary: Sketches the lives of the two men responsible for the first flight of a machine-powered aircraft on December 17, 1903, Kitty Hawk, North Carolina.
ISBN 1-56239-637-4
1. Wright, Orville, 1871-1948—Juvenile literature. 2. Wright, Wilbur, 1867-1912—Juvenile literature. 3. Aeronautics—United States—Biography—Juvenile literature. [1. Wright, Orville, 1871-1948. 2. Wright, Wilbur, 1867-1912. 3. Aeronautics--Biography.] I. Title. II. Series: Inventors (Series)
TL540.W7J67 1996
629.13'0092'273—dc20
[B]   95-49658
                                                           CIP
                                                            AC

Contents

Their First Flying Machine

In 1878, Milton Wright came home with a toy for his two young boys. Wilbur, 11, and Orville, 7, rushed to see what their father had brought for them. They looked at the toy and were puzzled. Their father showed them how it worked. Much to their amazement, the toy could fly! Their father told them that it was called a flying machine.

This toy **helicopter** was invented by Alphonse Penaud, a young Frenchman. It was made of bamboo, cork, and paper. Rubber bands, when wound, propelled the helicopter into the air.

In those days, there was no such thing as an airplane. So the young boys were very excited when they saw their toy fly. They played with it for many days.

Orville Wright.

Wilbur Wright.

The two boys looked at each other and knew what they wanted to do with their lives. "One day we will fly," said Wilbur.

"Yes," said Orville. "One day, we will."

The Early Years

Wilbur Wright was born April 16, 1867, near Millville, Indiana. His younger brother, Orville, was born August 19, 1871, in Dayton, Ohio.

The young boys were always trying to make their own toys, such as kites and toy cars. Both were excellent students. They loved to read and write, but neither could sit too long. They wanted to invent, design, and create things.

Neither attended college. Nor did they finish high school. Although their father wasn't happy with their decision, he knew they would make something of themselves because they were so smart and **innovative**.

The house where the Wright Brothers lived while they developed the first airplane in Dayton, Ohio.

Their First Jobs

In 1888, the two brothers started a **printing press**. The following year, they published the Dayton, Ohio, *West Side News*. Orville was the publisher and Wilbur was the editor.

Although the newspaper was successful, it kept them from working on flying machines. So they sold their business and opened a bicycle shop.

In just a few years, the bicycle shop was a huge success. Both brothers were gifted **mechanics** and could make or fix anything.

The Wright brothers designed a sturdy bike that could be made for less money than other bicycles. Soon they were selling enough bicycles to earn a very good living. Now they had free time during the winter months to concentrate on their number one hobby: the possibility of flying.

The Wright Cycle Company as it looks today in Greenfield, Michigan.

Birds and Kites

To study flight, the brothers watched birds that glided through the sky. They decided to design a **glider** they could ride. "We could not understand that there was anything about a bird that would enable it to fly that could not be built on a larger scale and used by man," said Orville.

To do this, the Wright brothers studied wind patterns. They also built kites that looked like small gliders. These kites were an unbelievable sight. Children from all over town would come and watch the brothers fly these kites. Even adults were amazed.

To keep the kites in the air as long as possible, the Wright brothers tried to control them from the ground. They knew that if a **pilot** were in control of a glider, that person could achieve much longer flights.

The Wright brothers had a few problems controlling the **glider**. Then Wilbur designed a **warped wing** that was curved on top. This gave the glider more control. Wilbur knew that when air flowed over a warped wing, it would produce the "lift" needed to get the glider off the ground.

Wilbur also knew that if a **pilot** could control the **warp** of each wing, the glider could be controlled and flown. If the glider dipped to the left, the pilot could increase the warp of the left wing. That would increase the lift of that wing and straighten out the craft.

The Wright brothers began working long hours, building a kite to test the warped wing design. The kite had a 5-foot (1.5-m) wing span. Lines hung down from the tip of each wing. With these lines, a person on the ground could control the wing warp. It worked perfectly! The brothers were very excited.

Gliders

In 1900, the Wright brothers built in their bicycle shop a **glider** that used wing **warping**. It was a big glider that one person could fly. The **pilot** would lie face down, looking at the ground, while holding two ropes that controlled the wings.

Now that the glider was ready, the brothers had to find the best place to fly it. Gliders need wind to get off the ground. So they needed a place where the wind blew almost constantly.

The Wright brothers chose a beach in North Carolina. There, a steady wind blew in from the Atlantic Ocean. The town was called Kitty Hawk. It had a 100-foot (30-m) sand dune. This was the perfect place to make their flight.

The brothers took turns flying the **glider**. Both discovered the thrill of flight. Lying face down, they watched the ground rush beneath them as their glider flew through the air.

Each tried the wing-**warping** system built into the glider. It worked better than they had expected! But their rides only lasted a short time, the longest being 10 seconds. They were determined to make a better glider.

The Wright brothers returned to Kitty Hawk in 1901 with a new and improved glider. This one broke the world record for glider flight by reaching 389 feet (119 m).

They still were not satisfied. The brothers believed they could go higher and for longer periods of time. After working another year on a new design, they returned to Kitty Hawk to try again.

The new craft had a **rudder** control. With their gliding experience, the Wright brothers had discovered they could get a more stable flight by combining wing **warping** with proper rudder movement.

With this new idea, the Wright brothers in 1902 soared more than 600 feet (183 m)–a new world record.

Opposite page:
One of the Wright brothers flying a glider at Kitty Hawk, North Carolina, in 1902.

***The Wright brothers' glider floating over the sand
dunes at Kitty Hawk.***

16

Dreamers?

The Wright brothers were the best at building **gliders**. But they wanted to fly an **engine**-powered air machine controlled by a **pilot**. This was something no one had ever done.

Many people thought their idea would never work. But some **scientists** and **engineers** believed that it could happen—including American scientist Samuel Pierpont Langley.

Langley made many models that flew. One was powered by a small steam engine and flew three-quarters of a mile (1.2 km) without a pilot.

The United States Army gave Langley $50,000 to continue his **experiments**. With the money, he hired many research assistants and bought modern equipment. Meanwhile, the Wright brothers worked alone, using the money from their bicycle shop to buy supplies.

On December 8, 1903, Langley was ready to try his airplane. He mounted the plane on rails which were fastened to the roof of a **houseboat** in the Potomac River. Receiving the signal to go, the **pilot** raced down the rails and nose-dived into the river.

It was a disaster for Langley and the United States Army. The Wright brothers were saddened to hear about Langley. They knew how hard he had worked. But Langley's failure did not stop the Wright brothers. They worked night and day to be the first to fly an **engine**-powered airplane.

*Samuel Langley's flying machine
after it crashed into the river.*

The Wright Brothers

1867
Wilbur Wright is born April 16th, in Millville, IN.

1871
Orville Wright is born August 19th, in Dayton, OH.

1888
Open a printing press.

1902
Glider soars 600 feet.

1903
The first powered airplane flight, Dec. 17th at Kitty Hawk, NC.

1908
The brothers set new distance and altitude records for flight.

Detail Area

Kitty Hawk

NORTH CAROLINA

Life & Invention Timeline

1892
Start
a bicycle
shop.

1900
Test their
glider at
Kill Devil Hills,
NC. Near Kitty
Hawk.

1901
Break world record
for glider flight
by reaching 389 feet
in Kitty Hawk,
NC.

1909
The brothers
form the
The Wright Co.
in Dayton, OH.

1912
Wilbur Wright
dies on May 30,
in Dayton, OH.

1948
Orville Wright
dies on Jan. 30th,
in Dayton, OH.

Detail Area

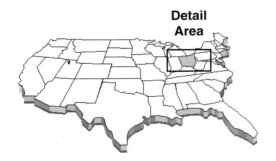

Making the Flyer

The Wright brothers knew they could make a flying machine. But they needed an **engine** light enough for flight. They wrote to several motor companies and discovered that none of them built the proper engine. So they had to build their own.

The brothers went to the library and studied engine design. Then they conducted many **experiments**. They finally made a 4-cylinder gasoline engine that weighed 150 pounds (68 kg).

The Wright brothers also designed a **propeller**, which they thought of as a moving wing. Their design had a curved top and a flat bottom.

Many **scientists**, including Langley, strongly disagreed with the design. But the Wright brothers were correct. Propellers today are built with the same design.

The Wright brothers spent many hours discussing and arguing the details of their airplane and how to fly it. As Orville once wrote, "Often, after an hour or so of heated argument, we would discover that we were as far from agreement as when we started, but that each of us had changed to the other's position."

By December 17, 1903, the arguing was over. The two brothers were ready to test their flying machine. They called it *Flyer I.*

The Flyer Flies

At 10:30 a.m., Wilbur started the **engine**. As the plane rumbled to life, the brothers shook hands. History was about to be made.

Orville climbed aboard *Flyer I* and lay face down alongside the engine on the lower wing. Then he signaled to his brother that he was ready.   *Flyer I* rolled forward—faster, and faster, and faster. Then suddenly, the plane lifted off the ground. Orville became the first person to fly an airplane.

That first flight carried Orville only 120 feet (37 m). Orville would later write, "The flight lasted only 12 seconds, but it was nevertheless the first time in the history of the world in which a machine carrying a man had raised itself by its own power into the air."

The brothers flew their aircraft three more times that day. On the last flight, Wilbur flew *Flyer I* 852 feet (260 m). The flight lasted 59 seconds.

The Wright brothers' first flight at Kitty Hawk, North Carolina, December 17, 1903. Orville is the pilot.

Innovative Brothers

The Wright brothers returned home to Dayton and continued to build and test more airplanes. Within a year, they had perfected an amazing airplane. It could fly 25 miles (40 km), stay in the air for 30 minutes, and had a top speed of 40 miles (64 km) per hour. The **pilot** had so much control, the plane could fly in circles and do figure eights.

Despite their success, the Wright brothers did not receive much attention until a newspaper reporter witnessed a 1,000-foot (305-m) flight in 1908. That same year, Wilbur traveled to France and flew their plane before European royalty.

*Opposite page: The Wright brothers' **Flyer I** takes flight.*

In 1909, the brothers formed the Wright Company. They opened a factory in Dayton to produce aircraft. Orders for their airplanes came from all over the world. Although they never designed planes for the money, the two became very wealthy.

Wilbur Wright did not live long enough to see the advances of air flight. He died in 1912 from typhoid fever. Orville Wright died in 1948, but he got to see the jet airplane and how it was used for both commercial and wartime use.

Through their hard work, dedication, and love of flight, the Wright brothers changed the world. The two **innovative** brothers will never be forgotten.

Opposite page:
The Wright Brothers
Monument near Kitty
Hawk, North Carolina.

Glossary

engine (EN-jun)- A piece of equipment that powers such things as a car or an airplane.

engineer (en-jun-NEAR) - Someone who designs a plan and sees that it is followed through.

experiment (ek-SPARE-uh-ment) - The process of testing in order to discover.

glider (GLI-der) - Something that looks like a small airplane but has no engine. It flies only by wind.

helicopter (HELL-uh-kop-ter) - A machine that flies in the air that is quite small whose support is only from one propeller.

houseboat - A very large boat that has a big deck and is able to be lived on.

innovative (IN-no-vay-tiv) - To come up with ideas and do things in a new way, a way that has never been done before.

mechanic (muh-CAN-ick) - A person who can fix many different types of machines.

pilot (PIE-lot) - The person who flies and controls the airplane.

printing press - A type of machine that prints such things as newspapers or magazines.

propeller (pro-PELL-er) - Usually three blades that are used as a moving wing on both sides of the airplane.

rudder (RUDD-er) - A piece attached to the back of the airplane that helps control direction of a flight.

scientist (SIGH-en-tist) - Someone very smart in science who studies and investigates questions and comes up with answers.

warp - To move by pulling on a line or cable.

warped wing - A wing that is curved at the top which gives control to the pilot and provides lift to the plane.

Index

jB
WRIGHT   Joseph, Paul.

                The Wright brothers.

$21.35

DATE			

BAKER & TAYLOR